THE C.C.C. CAMPS
IN WEST VIRGINIA

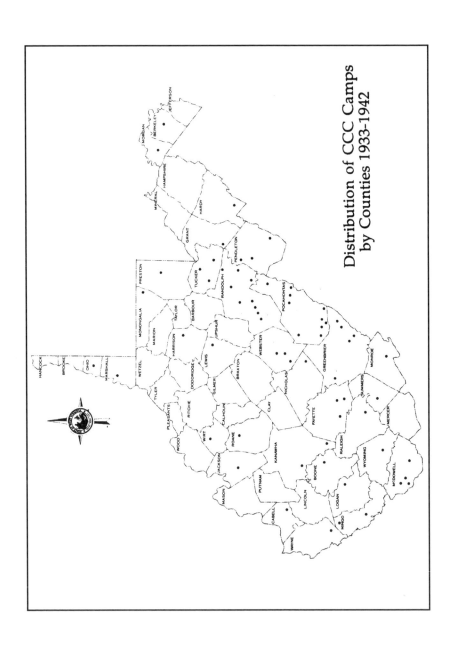

Distribution of CCC Camps
by Counties 1933-1942

THE C.C.C. CAMPS
IN
WEST VIRGINIA

A Record of the
Civilian Conservation Corps
in the Mountain State
1933-1942

MILTON HARR

Charleston, West Virginia

Library of Congress Card Catalog Number: 92-195216

ISBN-13: 978-1-891852-24-4
ISBN-10: 1-891852-24-8

First Edition

20 19 18 17 16 15 14 13 12 11 10 9 8 7 6

Originally published by Milton Harr.
Reprinted with permission by
Quarrier Press, Charleston, WV 25302.

Distributed by:

West Virginia Book Company
1125 Central Avenue
Charleston, WV 25302

www.wvbookco.com

TABLE OF CONTENTS

Camp Kanawha, S-76 on Kanawha State Forest 1938-1942
— Photo by Calvin White

FOREWORD

The Civilian Conservation Corps was born from the despair of the great depression when the nation was in desperate need of help and action.

When President Roosevelt took office in 1933 he faced a nation that was bankrupt in money and spirit. One of his first acts was to ask Congress for a large appropriation for emergency conservation work. This resulted in the passage, in March 1933, of the Emergency Work Act, or as it came to be called, the "Civilian Conservation Corps." It was a program to recruit thousands of young men to work in forests, parks, lands and water in the preservation and use of our basic natural resources.

The Civilian Conservation Corps was a result of Senate Bill 598 which the President had introduced March 27, 1933. The bill cleared both houses of Congress in four days and was on the President's desk for signature of March 31. The first CCC camp was opened in Virginia on April 17 and by July 1 there were 275,000 enrollees in 1,300 camps across the country.

Robert Fechner, a Boston labor leader, was appointed National Director by executive order 1601 on April 5, 1933. He established rules and regulations, allocated the funds, approved the establishment of camps and in general was responsible for the overall operation of the camps.

The U. S. Department of Labor chose a selection agent for each state to certify the selected enrollees to the War Department. On April 10, 1933, the first quota of 25,000 men was called, and on April 17 the first camp, Camp Roosevelt, located near Luray, Virginia on the George Washington National Forest, was occupied. Every state in the nation had one or more camps. The number of camps in a state depended on many factors, including the number of enrollees from that state and the number of projects that the state had readily available. Since there were not enough projects in the East to take care of the eastern men, many were sent to the western states.

The CCC program had an immediate economic impact. Supplies of all kinds from food to lumber, trucks, axes and shovels were required. The enrollees were required to send home $25.00 of the $30.00 monthly wage. The boost to the economy brought about by these checks was felt throughout the country.

There was a social impact. Young men were taken off the streets. They traveled far from home and performed useful work in a healthful environment and 40,000 illiterates learned to read and write. By 1935 600,000 enrollees were working out of 2,650 camps. By the time the program was disbanded in 1942 nearly three million men had engaged in this productive and popular program.

These men built fire towers, truck roads, firebreaks, planted millions of trees, reclaimed thousands of acres from erosion, built countless federal and state parks and campgrounds and improved fish and wildlife habitat.

Originally, enrollees were to be between the ages of 18 and 25 and from families on relief, but in 1935 the age requirement was raised to 28 and in 1937 the age limits were changed to 17 to 23 years and the relief requirement dropped.

By 1940, due to growing threat of war and the improvement in the nation's economy there were fewer than 200,000 men in about 900 camps. The need for the program was rapidly diminishing. Although Congress faced great pressure in 1942 to abolish the CCC, the Corps was never abolished. Congress simply failed to provide funds for its continuance, so after June 30, 1942 it officially went out of existence.

Kermit McKeever, Former Chief, Division of Parks and Recreation, W.Va. Dept. of Natural Resources

INTRODUCTION

Although much has been written about the Civilian Conservation Corps nationwide, very little is available on the CCC camps in West Virginia. It therefore seems desirable to record information on these camps while participants in the program are still available. In the pages that follow something is written about each camp established in West Virginia from 1933 to 1942. It is regretted that more information is not available for some camps and that exact locations for some cannot be given.

Seventy-two CCC camps were authorized for five agencies in West Virginia during the nine years the CCC program was in existence. Three of the authorized camps were not funded, so were not built, therefore, reducing the number of established camps to 69. In two other cases the camps were transferred from one agency to another and assigned a new camp number, resulting in one camp site having two camp designations. This reduces the number of camp sites to 67. One Forest Service camp, F-7 located on the George Washington National Forest and on the Virginia-West Virginia state line was assigned a West Virginia number by mistake and was later transferred to the Virginia list. This reduced the actual number of CCC camp sites in West Virginia to 66.

Of the five agencies sponsoring CCC camps in West Virginia, the U. S. Forest Service operated a total of twenty-two camps including two summer camps that were occupied only during the summer months.

The Division of Forestry of the Conservation Commission had twenty-six camps consisting of sixteen "P" camps working on private forest land and ten "S" camps on state forest land. The Division of State Parks of the Conservation Commission had eight camps including one on en area which later became a municipal park.

The U. S. Soil Conservation Service operated eleven camps which performed conservation work on private farms. The U. S. Army Corps of Engineers' only camp in West Virginia was located on Bluestone Reservoir.

The number of CCC camps in operation fluctuated from time to time so there probably were never more than two-thirds of the sixty-six camp sites occupied at any given time during the nine years the CCC existed.

ACKNOWLEDGMENTS

Most of the information for this publication was obtained by researching the records of the Civilian Conservation Corps on file in the National Archives in Washington, D. C. The staff of the Scientific, Economic and Natural Resources Branch was very helpful in selecting material to be studied. Additional information was obtained from annual reports of the Conservation Commission and the *W. Va. Blue Books* published between 1933 and 1942.

Other publications referred to include *The Tree Army* by Stan Cohen, *Roosevelt's Forest Army* by Perry Merrill and publications of the U. S. Forest Service and the National Association of Civilian Conservation Corps Alumni.

Individuals who furnished information include: Fredrick Armstrong, Charleston; Robert Beanblossom, Charleston; William L. Coffindaffer, Clarksburg; Nancy R. F. Feakes, USFS, Petersburg; Jack Feller, Mullens; D. P. "Sheriff" Given, Webster Springs; Kate Goodrich, USFS, Elkins; Charles R. Hall, Horner; Tommy Harbour, Milton; Donald G. Hebb, King wood; Hunter Lesser, USFS, Elkins; William McNeel, Marlinton; Ross Mellinger, Parkersburg; Walt Shupe, Huntersville; Homer J. Tennant, Solvang, Calif.; Robert Tennyson, Bridgewater, Va.; Calvin C. White, Charleston and James R. Wilkins, Winchester, Va.

I give special thanks to my wife Ida who typed and proofed copy and accompanied me on many field trips in search of CCC camp sites; to John G. Morgan, Charleston, who edited the material and to my sister Connie Peterson, St. Petersburg, Fla. who prepared the manuscript for printing.

A portion of Camp Glady Fork, F-2, a tent camp in 1933
— Photo by USPS – Monongahela National Forest

CAMP STRUCTURE AND ORGANIZATION

Each CCC camp consisted of a company of approximately 200 men. To administer the camp there was a staff consisting of a company commander, who was either a regular army officer or a reserve officer, a junior officer and an educational advisor. Each camp had the services of a camp doctor who was either a medical reserve officer or a contract physician from the area. In addition there was a project superintendent, employed by the technical service the camp was under, who was in charge of all work projects away from camp. He had a staff usually consisting of one engineer, one forester, one mechanic, one machine operator, one blacksmith and four foremen.

Many camps recruited "Local Experienced Men" or "L. E. M." to supervise the work crews and assist the technical staff. These "L. E. M." were usually older men with certain skills and experience in various crafts such as carpentry, stone work or woodcraft.

Enrollees were eligible to become "rated" men to help with the camp administration. Usually these "rated" men were senior leaders, mess stewards, storekeepers and cooks. In addition there were assistant leaders who were company clerks, assistant educational advisors and second cooks. These men were picked from the company roster and were paid $36 or $45 a month depending on their rating.

The average camp had 24 buildings consisting of a kitchen/mess hall, recreational building, educational building, infirmary, barracks for the enrollees and quarters for the officers and technical personnel. In the early days most camps began as a group of army pyramid or bell tents, housing four to six men each. The tents served until permanent buildings could be erected, usually by local contractors but sometimes by the enrollees themselves.

A permanent camp sometimes had one or more side or spike

1

camps set up for particular projects some distance from the base camp. These were usually tent camps used to house a small number of men.

A camp was identified by two official designations, the company number and the camp designation. The company number ususally indicated the Army Corps area in which the company was formed. The camp designation depended on the agency sponsoring it. For example, SP-4, Camp Morgan, was a state park sponsored camp (SP) and the fourth camp (4) set up by the Division of State Parks. In addition, each camp had an unofficial name decided on by the enrollees.

In the early days of the CCC there were some integrated companies containing a few black enrollees. Companies 523, 524, 525, 1524, and 2596 are examples of this. Later, separate companies for black youths were formed, with one such company being assigned to West Virginia. Most West Virginia CCC companies were junior companies with all white enrollees 18 to 25 years of age. Two companies, however, were designated as veterans' companies and were composed of veterans of World War I. Veterans' companies are indicated by a "V" following the company number and colored companies by a "C." Companies 1547V and 1558V were veterans' companies and 3538C was West Virginia's only colored company.

U. S. DEPARTMENT OF AGRICULTURE FOREST SERVICE

The U. S. Forest Service, which had been established in 1905, was responsible for the administration of the national forests, including two with lands in West Virginia. Its primary responsibilities were forest protection and timber management. All of the Monongahela National Forest and a portion of the George Washington National Forest are in West Virginia.

A total of twenty-four CCC camps were authorized for U. S. Forest Service use in West Virginia. One camp, F-21, however, intended for Pocahontas County was cancelled before construction could begin.

Of the above camps, twenty-two were authorized for and twenty-one actually put into service on the Monongahela National Forest. The other two were located in the George Washington National Forest. One of these, F-7 was on the Virginia-West Virginia state line. While initially counted as a West Virginia camp it was subsequently transferred to the State of Virginia list on March 24, 1934 as Camp F-15 (Va.). The other George Washington camp was Camp Little Fork, F-8 located in Pendleton County near Sugar Grove.

Forest Service camps contributed greatly to the protection and management of the forests, with CCC enrollees fighting forest fires, planting trees, thinning dense timber stands, collecting tree seeds, as well as working on forest recreation projects, blister rust control, insect and disease damage, road and trail construction and other projects related to forest management.

F-1, CAMP DRY FORK
5/20/33-11/11/33

Located in the Dry Fork-Red Creek area of Tucker County just north of W. Va. Rt. 32 at its junction with W. Va. Rt. 72 this tent camp was occupied May 20, 1933 by CCC Company 519, a junior company with an enrolled strength of 215. Ernest Smith was the camp superintendent.

The camp remained active through the summer but was abandoned about November 11, 1933 when Company 529 was transferred to Camp North Fork, F-11, on the North Fork of the South Branch of the Potomac River in Grant County.

F-2, CAMP GLADY FORK
5/26/33-12/15/37

Camp Glady Fork was located in Randolph County near the Tucker County line and just off the western edge of Otter Creek Wilderness Area. It was about five and a half miles north of Alpena P. O. and US Rt. 33. Situated on Glady Fork near its junction with Three Spring Run, at the point now occupied by the Otter Creek Campground, the camp was a short distance up Forest Service Rt. 162.

The camp was occupied May 26, 1933 by CCC Company 524 but was not approved for the fourth period (Oct. '34-March '35). It was evacuated November 10, 1934 and Company 524 moved to Camp Alvon, F-14 at Alvon. Camp F-2 was re-established for the fifth period (April-Sept. 1935) and occupied by Company 566 on June 14, 1935.

The camp was evacuated December 15, 1937 and Company 566 was disbanded and its members transferred to other companies. Later the camp site was utilized, at times, as a side camp. The last one was operated by 39 members of Camp Scott, F-24 during the summer of 1941.

Harry Wolfe and D.F. Christy were camp superintendants who administered the work projects. Capt. CD. Riggle and Capt. Virgil E. Buriss were company commanders.

F-3, CAMP PARSONS
4/20/33-1942

Located in Tucker County, just east of Parsons and adjacent to the

Forest Service tree nursery, this camp was occupied May 20, 1933 by CCC Company 518 with 206 enrollees, all recruited in West Virginia. The primary project for the camp involved work in the tree nursery.

Early camp superintendents include Harold Hebb, H. K. Burrell, E. R. Sutton and John King.

Camp Parsons remained in service throughout the life of the CCC program until it was abandoned in 1942.

F-4, CAMP LAUREL FORK
5/20/33-7/10/37

Camp Laurel Fork was located in Randolph County about twelve miles south of Wymer P. O. and U.S. Rt. 33. Situated on the present site of Laurel Fork Campground near the headwaters of Laurel Fork, the site can be reached by way of Forest Service Rt. 14 (Middle Mountain Road) for ten miles, thence two miles on Forest Service Rt. 423.

This camp was occupied May 20, 1933 by CCC Company 520 with an enrolled strength of 191. The broad work program covered forest protection and improvement work in the Cheat District of the Monongahela National Forest.

Funding was not approved for the tenth period (Oct. '37-Mar. '38) so the camp was abandoned July 10, 1937 and the camp buildings transferred to the U. S. Forest Service.

Of the original camp buildings, a 30 X 30 foot one story structure remains. Originally used as CCC personnel quarters, it now serves as the wildlife manager's residence for the Beaverdam Wildlife Management Unit.

F-5, CAMP CIRCLEVILLE
5/26/33-11/10/33

This camp was located in Pendleton County at the junction of W.V. Rt. 28 and U. S. Rt. 33 near Judy Gap and was occupied May 26, 1933 by CCC Company 523. Records are sparse, however, it is believed that it was a temporary tent camp which occupied the site for only one summer, closing November 10,1933, when Company 523 was transferred to Camp Kanawha, P-59, Decota.

F-6, CAMP THORNWOOD
5/26/33-1942

Located on W. Va. Rt. 28 two miles north of U. S. Rt. 250 junction, on the present site of Pocahontas County 4-H Camp, it was occupied as a tent camp May 26,1933 by CCC Company 521 which remained for about six months. On or about November 20, 1933 Company 521 was transferred to Camp Woodbine, F-12, Richwood.

After being closed for about a year and a half, Camp Thornwood was reestablished and occupied July 1, 1935 by CCC Company 2586, which remained until the camp was closed in 1942.

George Fry and Peter J. Hanlon were listed as camp superintendents.

F-7, CAMP WOLF GAP
5/15/33-3/24/34

Located in Hardy County in the George Washington National Forest, this camp was occupied May 15,1933 by CCC Company 333 as a tent camp with permanent barracks being completed later in the year.

The first company commander was 1st Lt. Kent J. Nelson who was succeeded by Capt. LeRoy H. Barnard on September 16.

The camp was situated on the Virginia-West Virginia state line in the vicinity of the present Wolf Gap Recreation Area. Most of the Army buildings were on the Virginia side and the Forest Service facilities and repair shops were on the West Virginia side.

The work projects under the supervision of Camp Superintendent James R. Wilkins, included road and trail construction, timber stand improvement, fire control, tree planting, surveying and other similar jobs, most of which were in West Virginia.

On March 24, 1934 the camp was redesignated F-15 Virginia, since it was determined that the camp had been carried in West Virginia by mistake and should have been originally listed with the state of Virginia.

F-8, CAMP LITTLE FORK
6/18/33-12/1/37

This George Washington National Forest camp was located in Pendleton County about two miles east of Sugar Grove P. O. at the northeast corner of the U. S. Naval Reservation. Camp Little Fork was beside Little Fork of the South Branch of the Potomac River, about a half mile up county Rt. 24 from its junction with county Rt. 25. It was occupied June 18,1933 by CCC Company 1523 consisting of 204 enrollees, most of whom were from Ohio with a few West Virginians. In April 1935 this company was replaced by CCC Company 2587.

Primary work projects included road construction, timber stand improvement, timber estimation surveys as well as forest fire fighting.

A. C. Dahl was camp superintendent and the following were company commanders: Ensign Christopher C. Vierling and 2nd Lt. Chester J. Kulakoski. First Lt. Maurice Hymen, Medical Reserve was camp doctor.

The camp is believed to have been abandoned in December 1937.

F-9, CAMP RANDOLPH (1st.)
5/26/33-11/20/33

Located in Randolph County about four miles east of Elkins and just north of U.S. Rt. 33 on the present site of Stuart Recreation Area, this camp was occupied as a tent camp by CCC Company 525 on May 26,1933. An integrated company, 525 had 189 white and 14 black enrollees.

Camp F-9 was not approved nor funded for the second period (Oct. '33-Mar. '34) so after about six months of operation it was abandoned and Company 525 was moved to Camp Cranberry, F-13 in Webster County.

F-10, CAMP LEADMINE
6/18/33-5/15/34

Located in Tucker County, southwest of Lead Mine Post Office on Horseshoe Run on the present site of YMCA Camp Horseshoe and near the Horseshoe Recreation Area, the camp was occupied as a tent camp June 18,1933 by CCC Company 1524 with a strength of 221 enrollees, 26 from West Virginia and 195 from Ohio.

Since the camp was not approved for the third period (April-Sept. 1934) it is believed that the camp was abandoned in April 1934, when Company 1524 was transferred to Camp Hardy, SP-2 on Lost River State Park.

F-11, CAMP NORTH FORK
10/10/33-1942

Camp North Fork was located on the North Fork of the South Branch of the Potomac River in the Crows Ridge section of Grant County. The camp site is about 200 feet west of W. Va. Rt. 28 at a point where a CCC roadside memorial marker has been erected, one mile north of the Pendleton County line. One original CCC building remains on the site.

The camp was established October 10 and occupied November 18, 1933 by CCC Company 519 which had been transferred from Camp Dry Fork, F-1, Tucker County. The company occupied permanent camp buildings of the rigid type rather than tents as at their previous site.

Major projects consisted of truck trail construction, maintenance of fire trails, timber estimating, telephone line construction, recreational camp construction and forest fire suppression on the national forest.

On July 11, 1940 Company 519 moved to Camp Scott, F-24 a summer camp, but returned to F-11 on November 4 for the winter. On April 5,1941 Company 519 again evacuated F-11 and reoccupied F-24 for the summer, returning November 14. During the summer months Camp F-ll was maintained as a side camp with about fifteen enrollees.

Capt. Merrill G. Beck and Lt. Manning Fenrich were company

8

commanders and Enos Kerns and Charles P. Mauzy were camp superintendents.

It is believed that Camp North Fork was last abandoned about mid-1942 when the Civilian Conservation Corps went out of existence.

F-12, CAMP WOODBINE
11/20/33-10/23/35

Located in Nicholas County about five miles north of Rich wood beside the Cranberry River on the present site of Woodbine Picnic Area, this camp was occupied November 20,1933 by CCC Company 521. This was a junior company with 192 white enrollees, all from West Virginia except for two from Ohio.

The work projects included those common to the other Forest Service camps on the Monongahela National Forest, including fire fighting, road and trail building and timber stand improvement.

The camp, which was not approved for the sixth period (Oct. '35-Mar. '36) was abandoned October 23,1935. It was dismantled in 1939-40 and the buildings transferred to the U. S. Forest Service.

G.R. Willis was company commander and J. A. Helm was camp superintendent.

F-13, CAMP CRANBERRY
11/20/33-1942

Said to have been the most isolated CCC camp in West Virginia, Camp Cranberry was located in Webster County about three miles from the Nicholas County line, and about five miles NNE of Rich wood and five miles SSW of Webster Springs. It was between Cranberry River and Forest Service Road 76 at the mouth of Aldrich Creek and about a mile west of the Cranberry Recreation Area. The camp was occupied November 20,1933 by CCC Company 525, which had been moved from Camp F-9 near Elkins when that camp was abandoned.

Camp Cranberry, which had been in service throughout the CCC program, is believed to have been abandoned in 1942 when the Civilian

Conservation Corps went out of existence.

E.S. Evans and John L. Gillis were camp superintendents, and Emick R. Halls was one of the last company commanders.

F-14, CAMP ALVON
11/10/34-12/4/35

Camp Alvon was located in Greenbrier County on Anthony Creek between Alvon and Blue Bend Recreation Area at the present site of Camp Wood, the summer camp for WVU Department of Geology, which still uses several of the original CCC buildings.

The camp was occupied November 10,1934 by CCC company 524 which had transferred from Camp Glady Fork, F-2 Alpena, Randolph County.

Capt. A. S. Anderson and Capt. Clifford M. Cotts were company commanders and E. L. Miller and P. A. Bittinger were camp superintendents.

Records show that the camp was not approved for the sixth period (Oct. '35-Mar. '36) and was abandoned December 4, 1935. Company 524 was moved to Camp Bluestone, C of E-l and the camp buildings transferred to the Forest Service who maintained them and renamed the camp, Camp Wood, in honor of Arthur A. Wood, supervisor of the Monongahela National Forest from 1931 to 1949.

Under a special use permit the camp was made available to West Virginia University and was used in the summer of 1937 by the Forestry School for its summer camp. Subsequently the camp was used by the Geology Department in its summer program.

F-15, CAMP BLACK MOUNTAIN
7/11/35-1941

Located in Pocahontas County on Williams River above the mouth of Big Laurel Creek near the western boundary of the Handley Public Hunting and Fishing Area, the camp was occupied July 11, 1935 by CCC Company 2589. One report, however lists August 26, 1935 as the date the camp was established. As with most of the early camps, the buildings were of the rigid rather than the portable type.

This was a white junior camp with practically all the enrollees from West Virginia. Being a Forest Service camp on the Monongahela National Forest the work consisted of the usual type of projects including road and trail construction, fire control and forest management activities.

The camp was temporarily shut down in March 1939 but was reoccupied May 10,1941 for a brief period, with CCC Company 2590 which had been transferred from Camp Anthony, F-18, Neola. The last inspection report on file for Camp F-15 was dated July 23, 1941 which indicates that the camp was probably abandoned late in 1941.

An inspection report dated May 16, 1938 reported that this camp had charge of a side camp of thirty enrollees located near Slaty Fork on Old Field Fork of Elk River at the mouth of Roaring Run. The side camp, about twenty miles from Camp F-15 had been established in July 1937 and was expected to continue indefinitely.

Capt. Wilfred Jackson and James A. Riley were company commanders and William C. Kramer and Ernest F. Smith were camp superintendents.

F-16, CAMP NICHOLAS
7/1/35-1/8/36

Located in Webster County between Williams River and County Highway 46 about four miles east of its junction with W. Va. Rt. 20, Camp Nicholas was originally established as a private forestry camp operated by the Conservation Commission's Division of Forestry primarily for forest fire control activities on privately owned forest land

After transfer to the U. S. Forest Service it was reoccupied July 1,1935 by CCC Company 2591. Since funds were not approved for the sixth period (Oct. '35-Mar. '36) the camp was abandoned January 8,1936 and the buildings transferred to the Forest Service.

Capt. H. E. Pool was company commander and D. J. Parsons and Wayland Feamster were camp superintendents.

F-17, CAMP COPPERHEAD
7/10/35-10/4/37

Located in Pocahontas County one mile east of Frost on W. Va. Rt. 84 at Bird Run and the present site of the Bird Run Recreation Area, this camp was occupied July 10,1935 by CCC Company 3539. The name was chosen because of the many copperhead snakes believed to be in the area.

An August 1935 inspection report stated that the camp site was originally occupied by a cadre of 23 men from Company 566, Camp Glady Fork, F-2 on July 10, 1935 with an additional 166 enrollees arriving later in July to form CCC Company 3539. The men were quartered in tents in the beginning, but on September 1,1935 began the erection of portable camp buildings which had been fabricated at the factory.

Lt. Carlton G. Hine was company commander and John Gillis and Del J. Parsons were camp superintendents.

Since funds were not authorized for the tenth period (Oct. '37-Mar. '38) the camp was abandoned October 4, 1937 and the camp buildings shipped to the 8th Corps Area, Carlsbad, New Mexico.

F-18, CAMP ANTHONY
8/19/35-3/16/42

Located at Neola in Greenbrier County north of W. Va. Rt. 92 and across the highway from the present site of the Anthony Correctional Center, this camp, with portable type buildings, was occupied August 19,1935 by CCC Company 2590.

As with other U. S. Forest Service camps, on the Monongahela National Forest, the work generally included forest fire suppression, road and trail construction and timber stand improvement.

On May 9, 1941 Company 2590 was transferred to Camp Black Mountain, F-15, Marlinton, where it remained for the summer. Then on November 1,1941 Company 2590 returned to Camp Anthony where it remained until it was transferred to Camp Stonewall Jackson, SCS-12,

Jane Lew, March 16, 1942. Since Camp Anthony had not been approved for the next work period it is presumed to have been abandoned March 16, 1942 with the transfer of its last CCC company.

Capt. Arthur S. Rothrock and Jules G. Kiplinger were listed as company commanders and Del J. Parsons and Ernest F. Smith were camp superintendents.

F-19, CAMP LORING
7/25/35-10/4/37

Located in Pocahontas County on Cochran Creek at Rimel at the junction of W. Va. Routes 92 and 39, this U. S. Forest Service camp was occupied July 25,1935 by CCC Company 2596. After only five months in camp, this company was replaced January 11, 1936 by CCC Company 1580 which had been transferred from Camp Jackson, SCS-6, Ripley.

The camp was named for Brig. Gen. William Loring, commander of the Confederate Army of the Northeast with headquarters at Huntersville in 1861 during the Civil War.

A report dated August 2, 1935 stated that the men were quartered in tents and that construction had not yet started on the new portable buildings which were to come prefabricated from the factory.

Camp officials included Capt. L. H. Headington and 1st Lt. Harold L. Short who were company commanders, M. C. Gatewood and E. R. Sutton camp superintendents and Asher W. Kelly, Jr. a squad foreman who was later to become state forester of W. Va. in the 1970s.

Since the camp was not approved for the tenth period (Oct. '37-Mar/38) it was abandoned October 4,1937 and the camp buildings were later shipped to the 8th Corps Area, Roswell, New Mexico.

F-20, CAMP WHITE
7/1/35-10/4/37

Located in Pendleton County about one half mile up Seneca Creek where it leaves U. S. Rt. 33, about two miles west of Onego, this camp was named for Whites Run which flows into Seneca Creek about a mile above the camp. The camp site is near the present Seneca Recreation Area, a small campground on the north boundary of the Spruce Knob Unit of the Spruce Knob-Seneca Rocks National Recreation Area

Camp White was occupied July 1,1935 by CCC Company 2595 and the enrollees were still quartered in tents as of July 27. Camp buildings, however, were under construction and scheduled for completion by fall

Capt. James G. Graham was company commander and Joseph A. Helm was camp superintendent.

The camp was not approved for the tenth period (Oct. '37-Mar. '38) so it was abandoned October 4, 1937 and the camp buildings transferred to the U. S. Forest Service.

F-21...

A Forest Service camp was authorized for location in Pocahontas County but was canceled before construction began.

F-22, CAMP HUTTON
7/10/35-1938

Camp Hutton was located in Randolph County at the foot of Cheat Mountain about 1 mile up Forest Service Route 26 from its junction with U. S. Route 250 about three miles south of Huttonsville Medium Security Prison. The camp was occupied July 10, 1935 by CCC Company 2597. This was a junior company with 160 enrollees on December 31, 1936, of which 149 were from West Virginia and eleven from Ohio.

Company commanders included Capt. H. T. Burnham, 1st Lt. Frederick F. Riley and 2nd Lt. Everett K. Shimp. Camp superintendents were Everett Taylor and Carl C. Hertig.

The last inspection report on file for this camp was dated May 12,1938 so it is believed that the camp was abandoned sometime in 1938.

F-23, CAMP CHEAT MOUNTAIN
7/11/40-10/1/41

Camp Cheat Mountain was located in Randolph County on the western edge of Cheat Mountain, four miles out Forest Service Route 92 from its junction with U. S. Route 250 at the top of Cheat Mountain. Located just off the right side of the road about a quarter mile south of its junction with Forest Service Route 47 the camp site is now a grassy wildlife opening with only a few concrete forms that denote the location of the CCC camp.

This camp was first occupied July 11,1940 as a summer camp by CCC Company 2586, the company assigned to Camp Thornwood, F-6. In the late fall the company returned to its permanent camp, F-6 for the winter.

The camp consisted of portable type buildings for the mess hall, combination education building/recreation hall and bathhouse and tents instead of barracks. Apparently the camp was again occupied during the next summer, but was permanently abandoned in the fall of 1941.

E. M. Dews was listed as company commander and Woodrow W. Lee as subaltern. Peter J. Hanlan was the camp superintendent.

F-24, CAMP SCOTT
7/11/40-11/4/40 & 4/15/41-11/14/41

Camp Scott was located in Randolph County just west of the southern tip of the Spruce Knob-Seneca Rocks National Recreation Area and in the vicinity of Taylor and Pharis Knobs near the mouth of Big Run. It was situated west of Gandy Creek and WV Secondary Rt. 29 about eight miles south of Whitmer P. O. which in turn is about eight miles south of U. S. Rt. 33. It is said to have been named for the Scott White family.

The camp was first occupied July 11, 1940 as a sumer camp by CCC Company 519, the company regularly assisgned to Camp North Fork, F-11.

The camp consisted of nine buildings, three rigid and six portable, and included the mess hall, bathhouse, offices, combination recreational hall/education building, technical service garage and utility buildings. Enrollees were quartered in tents.

The camp was occupied until November 4 at which time the company returned to Camp North Fork for the winter. On April 15, 1941, Camp F-24 was again occupied for the summer with Company 519 remaining there until November 14, 1941, when the camp was abandoned for the last time and the company returned to Camp F-11

During the summer fifteen enrollees remained at Camp F-11 as a side camp and thirty-nine men maintained another side camp at Camp Glady Fork, F-2, Alpena.

H.K. Burrell and Samuel B. Kromberg served as camp superintendents. C.C. Albaugh, Jr. and W.D. Scroggin were company commanders and Martin Hofstetter was subaltern.

View east, Civilian Conservation Corps Camp Parsons garage,
modern shed, and blacksmith shop.
— Library of Congress Reproduction Number HABS WVA,47-PARS.V,1--8

W. VA. CONSERVATION COMMISSION
DIVISION OF FORESTRY

The Forestry Division of the Conservation Commission in cooperation with the U. S. Forest Service operated CCC camps on both private and state owned forest land.

Regulations required that all work carried out on private forest land by these camps must have a direct bearing on and be of a forest fire protection nature. In West Virginia the majority of work consisted of motor truck trail construction, horse trail construction, fire tower erection, bridge construction, prevention of forest fires, fighting forest fires, telephone line construction, ranger station construction and fire hazard reduction.

In addition to the above projects, the CCC camps on state owned forestland did boundary survey, forest stand improvement, lake and dam construction, stream improvement, landscaping, tree planting, game survey, game protection and vermin control.

Twenty-seven CCC camps were authorized for the Division of Forestry, however only twenty-six were actually established. Camp P-69 was authorized but not funded or built.

Of these twenty-six CCC camps which actually operated, sixteen were on private forest land and were designated as "P" camps. The ten camps located on or working on state forest land were designated as "S" camps.

Three of these camps were initially "P" camps but were redesignated as "S" camps when they were assigned work on state forests. These camps were: Camp White Sulphur (from P-67 to S-67), Camp Twelvepole (from P-71 to S-71) and Camp Randolph (from P-72 to S-72).

The number of camps fluctuated from one work period to the next. The Division of Forestry's seven camps for the first period (Apr.-Sept.

1933) dropped to a low of three camps for the fourth work period (Oct. '34-Mar. '35) and rose to a high of twenty camps for the fifth period (Apr.-Sept. 1935).

Following are listed all of the CCC camps administered by the Division of Forestry during the entire life of the CCC program from May 1933 through June 1942.

S-51, CAMP SENECA
6/22/33-5/31/38

Located in Seneca State Forest in Pocahontas County at the junction of W. Va. Rt. 28 and the Seneca Lake Road, this camp was occupied, as a tent camp, June 22, 1933 by CCC Company 1537. Winter quarters were completed January 5, 1934, east of Rt. 28 and opposite the present forest headquarters.

Work projects for the camp included construction of truck trails, forest stand improvement, reduction of fire hazards and construction of eight log cabins for rental to the public. Two large cabins were located on Greenbrier River and six smaller ones on the shore of Seneca Lake.

R. W. Griffith was camp superintendent and Capt. E. R. Howery was company commander.

The camp was abandoned May 31, 1938 and Company 1537 transferred to Camp White Sulphur Springs, P-67 (later S-67) on Harfs Run in Greenbrier County.

S-52, CAMP WATOGA
6/18/33-8/15/34

Located on Beaver Creek near the entrance to Watoga State Forest this camp was occupied June 18, 1933 by CCC Company 1525. The camp enrollees were housed in tents while the more permanent camp buildings were being erected, such as the barracks which were completed by November 20,1933.

Work projects under the Division of Forestry included fire hazard reduction and blister rust control.

After fourteen months of operation the camp was transferred

August 15, 1934 to the National Park Service when Watoga became a state park under the management of the Division of State Parks of the West Virginia Conservation Commission. Camp Watoga was then designated as SP-5.

Captain LeGrand H. Headington was the company commander and S. E. Neese the camp superintendent.

P-53, CAMP NICHOLAS
7/18/33-5/1/34

Located in Webster County on County Highway 46 about four miles east of its junction with W. Va. Rt. 20 between Cowen and Upper Glade, Camp Nicholas was situated on a level area between Rt. 46 and Williams River. The camp was occupied July 18, 1933, as a tent camp, by CCC Company 1547V, a company of World War I veterans. It was operated by the W. Va. Conservation Commission's Division of Forestry primarily for forest fire control on privately owned forest land.

The last inspection report on file, dated March 28, 1934, indicated the camp was to be abandoned as a state camp around the first of May 1934 since it was not approved for the third period (April-Sept. 1934).

The camp was reestablished for the fifth period (April-Sept. 1935), and was turned over to the U. S. Forest Service and occupied July 1, 1935 as Camp F-16.

Capt. George R. Kyle served as company commander and Robert L. Porter was camp superintendent.

P-54, CAMP WYOMING
6/22/33-4/30/36

Camp Wyoming was located in Wyoming County about one mile west of Pineville on WV Rt. 97 on land leased from the W. M. Ritter Lumber Co. The camp, situated on the present site of Mullensville, was occupied June 22, 1933 by CCC Company 1538. The men were housed in tents until late autumn when permanent wooden barracks were ready for occupancy.

The first work project was the building of a road to Lambert Knob Fire Tower. Other work included fire suppression and the construction of roads, fire trails and four cabins for use as ranger stations.

The camp was not approved for the seventh period (April-Sept. 1936) so it was abandoned April 30, 1936 and the camp buildings returned to the W. M. Ritter Lumber Co.

Following closure of the camp two or three of the old CCC camp barracks buildings were converted to one or two family dwellings which were privately owned. Abandoned after several years of such use the buildings deteriorated and by 1991 only one remained as a derelict.

Capt. Charles W. Mays was the first company commander, followed by Capts. G.V. Biggs and John P. West. Rush Cozart and J.N. Wittenberg were camp superintendents.

P-55, CAMP BOONE
6/22/33-4/7/38

Camp Boone was located in Boone County on private land just east of WV Rt. 3 at the mouth of Stover Branch Hollow, one-half mile south of Keith P. O. and about three miles north of Sylvester. The site is presently leased to the Whitesville Gun Club by the current landowner.

The camp was occupied June 22, 1933, as a tent camp, by CCC Company 1540. Permanent buildings were made available later in the year.

The enrollees performed forest fire protection work on private forest land within a radius of twenty-five miles of the camp.

Since the camp was not approved for the fourth period (Oct. '34 - Mar. '35) it was vacated October 3, 1934. On July 2, 1935 the camp was reoccupied—this time by CCC Company 2599 which remained until April 7, 1938 when P-55 was abandoned and the company transferred to Camp Kanawha in Kanawha State Forest.

During the time Camp Boone was in operation it was served by three company commanders: Capt. Raymond Calton, Capt. John P. West and 1st Lt. M. M. Brown. Camp superintendents included C. E. Barrett, J. Ligon Coyner and Donald L. Lord.

P-56, CAMP POCAHONTAS
6/23/33-10/28/35

Initially called Camp Randolph, this camp was located in Pocahontas County two miles west of Cass at the junction of Back Mountain and Cold Run Roads. It was occupied June 23, 1933 as a tent camp by CCC Company 1535. Barracks were completed and occupied February 15, 1934. The main project was the building of a road, now known as the CCC Road, to Linwood.

Company 1535 remained at Camp Pocahontas until October 4, 1934 when it was transferred to Camp Seebert, SP-1 on Watoga State Park.

Camp Pocahontas was not approved for the fourth period (Oct. '34-March '35) so the camp stood vacant from October 4,1934 until it was reoccupied by CCC Company 2588 July 1, 1935. Since it was not approved for the sixth period (Oct. '35-March 36) the camp was abandoned October 28, 1935 and the following disposition made of the buildings: five were salvaged for CCC use by the Forest Service and the remaining 13 were cleared for sale March 19, 1937.

Camp superintendents were Noah Moore and J. Ligon Coyner while company commanders were Capt. Fred Klenk and Capt. Virgil E. Burriss.

P-57, CAMP GREENBRIER
6/23/33-1/11/36

Located on private land in Greenbrier County on U. S. Route 60 at Hines the camp was occupied June 23,1933 as a tent camp by CCC Company 1539. The permanent camp was under construction during the fall, and winter quarters were completed and occupied December 15, 1933.

Funds were not approved for the fourth period (Oct. '34-Mar. '35) so the camp stood vacant for about six months before being reestablished July 1, 1935 and occupied by CCC Company 2593. The camp was not approved for the sixth period (Oct. '35-Mar. '36) so it appears that Company 2593 was there through the fall of 1935. Records indicate that the camp was last abandoned January 11, 1936 and the buildings salvaged for CCC use.

Company commanders include C. R. Hoffecker, Lt, USNR and Capt. Harold R. Kelley. F. W. Pickering and W. T. Henshaw, Jr. were camp superintendents.

P-58, CAMP LOGAN
7/18/33-1941

Camp Logan was located in Logan County about two miles south of Sharpies on the east side of WV Rt. 17 (Old US 119) at the mouth of Seng Camp Hollow. This camp was occupied July 18,1933 by CCC Company 1558V, a veterans company of World War I veterans. The stone entrance across the highway from Sharpies High School is all that remains of the camp structures.

Work projects for this camp involved forest protection work including fire suppression on private land in Logan and Boone counties.

Since P-58 was not approved for the twelfth period (Oct. '38-Mar. '39) the camp was evacuated October 20, 1938 and Company 1558V was moved to Camp Anthony Wayne, S-61 on Cabwaylingo State Forest. It remained there until April 11, 1939 when Camp S-61 was evacuated leaving a small detachment to maintain a side camp. Company 1558V then returned to Camp Logan where it remained until the camp was abandoned late in 1941.

Company commanders included Capt. F. L. Boaz, Capt. James G. Graham, 1st Lt. Jesse A. Beck and B. J. Shinn, Lt. U. S. Navy. Raymond Parks, C. Earl Mullins and Richard Dunkle were camp superintendents.

P-59, CAMP KANAWHA (1st)
11/10/33-1/8/36

Located in Kanawha County on Cabin Creek near Decota, this private forest camp was occupied November 10, 1933 by CCC Company 523 which had been transferred from Camp Circleville, F-5,

Pendleton County. Company 523 remained at Camp Kanawha until October 1934 when the camp was closed due to not being approved for the fourth period (Oct. '34-Mar. '35).

The camp was re-established July 1, 1935 and occupied by CCC Company 3513 which stayed there until January 8,1936 when Camp P-59 was abandoned and the buildings disposed of as follows: Eight buildings were salvaged for CCC use and the balance were cleared for sale.

Capt. J. T. Smoody and Capt Franklin W. Patten were company commanders and J. B. Given and E. O. Fling were camp superintendents.

P-60, CAMP OAK HILL
5/15/34-10/10/34

Located on private land in Fayette County near enough to Oak Hill to obtain city water, this tent camp was occupied May 15, 1934 by CCC Company 1547V which had been transferred from Camp Nicholas, P-53, Cowen, W. Va. The company consisted of 178 white veterans.

The camp was not approved for the fourth period (Oct. '34-Mar. '35) so Company 1547V was transferred to Camp Roane, SCS-1, Reedy, on October 10, 1934 and Camp P-60 was abandoned and the few buildings were transferred to FERA.

Capt. George R. Kyle was the company commander and Robert L. Porter the camp superintendent.

S-61, CAMP ANTHONY WAYNE
7/4/35-4/11/39

Located near the mouth of Sweetwater Branch of Twelvepole Creek in Wayne County on the present site of the youth camp in Cabwaylingo State Forest, the camp was occupied July 4, 1935 by CCC Company 3532, which remained until October 20, 1938. Construction of camp buildings, which were of the rigid type, was completed August 23, 1935.

Cabwaylingo State Forest, of approximately 7,000 acres, had been purchased in February 1935. Camp S-61 was one of two CCC camps allocated for development work on the state forest.

Development projects included timber stand improvement, game refuge development, forest fire protection consisting of construction of a fire tower, telephone lines, ranger stations and truck trails. Later work included construction of thirteen vacation rental log cabins.

On October 20, 1938, Company 3532 was replaced by Company 1558V, a company of World War I veterans, which had been transferred from Camp Logan, P-58. This company remained there until April 11, 1939 when Camp Anthony Wayne was abandoned.

Camp superintendents serving the camp included William Osborne, C. E. Barrett and C. Earl Mullins. Company commanders were Capt. John Enochs, Capt. R. E. Kemp and 1st Lt. Leland C. Tennant.

S-62, CAMP BOWERS
7/1/35-1941

Located at the head of Mill Creek in Randolph County and on Kumbrabow State Forest, the camp was occupied July 1, 1935 by CCC Company 2594. Camp Bowers, which had the distinction of being located at the highest elevation of any CCC camp in West Virginia, was one of two camps allocated for work on Kumbrabow State Forest, for which the land had been purchased in December 1934. The other camp was Camp Randolph, S-72 at Elkwater. Work projects included carrying out the function of a game refuge, timber production and recreational development.

George Harris was camp superintendent and in his absence due to illness Frank O. Frazier was acting superintendent. Capt. Thomas M. Barton, 1st Lt. Thomas V. Cogan, Ensign Alexander M. Gray and 1st Lt. Harold Short were company commanders.

Although the camp was scheduled to close March 31, 1940, this did not happen since it was still in operation during the winter of 1940-41. It probably closed in the fall of 1941.

P-63, CAMP WAR
7/11/35-11/4/41

Located on private land in McDowell County about five miles east of War, on WV Rt. 16 and on the western edge of the town of Cucumber, the camp was occupied July 11, 1935 by CCC Company 3538C consisting of black junior enrollees.

The work projects included forest fire protection, construction and maintenance of truck trails, maintenance of telephone lines and fighting forest fires.

An inspection report indicates that P-63 was scheduled to be abandoned July 1, 1941 but was kept operating until November 8, at which time Company 3538C was transferred to Camp Carver, S-77, on Panther State Forest.

Capt. Art H. Bristow, Capt. L. H. Headington and Lt. J. H. Stamper, Jr. were listed as company commanders and Fred C. Hardman, R. G. Thornburg, Donald L. Lord and Barnes E. Hall were camp superintendents.

A report dated August 18, 1941 referred to a side camp at Panther W. Va. with an officer, two technical service foremen and 53 enrollees. This cadre apparently was getting the new Camp S-77 in readiness for the complete company's arrival November 8.

P-64, CAMP MCDOWELL
7/25/35-5/31/37

This McDowell County camp was established on private forest land on Panther Creek at the mouth of Trace Fork by the arrival on July 25, 1935 of a cadre of 25 enrollees from Carrollton, Kentucky. Then on August 8 the camp was occupied, as a tent camp, by 170 enrollees of CCC Company 3543. With materials arriving and the company at full strength, construction started immediately.

An October 17, 1935 inspection report advised that construction of the portable type camp buildings was 98% complete and that the enrollees were quartered in barracks. It was later reported that all camp buildings were completed by October 29.

The work program for this camp consisted of projects related to forest fire protection on the surrounding private forest land.

The camp was not approved for the tenth period (Oct. '37-Mar. '38), however one report indicates that the camp was abandoned earlier—on May 31, 1937 and the buildings disposed of. Some were shipped to the 8th Corps Area, Sunbeam, Colorado and the remaining nine were cleared for sale.

Capt. H. R. Bobb, 1st Lt. Charles L. Lockhart and Capt. Jas. E. Wilkins were company commanders and A. A. Price and D. K. Flynn were camp superintendents.

P-65, CAMP PANTHER
4/1/35-10/19/35

This camp was located in McDowell County on private land about 3 1/2 miles up Panther Creek from the mouth of Trace Fork and was occupied, as a tent camp, by CCC Company 3534 in April 1935.

A few months later another CCC camp, Camp McDowell, P-64 was established at the mouth of Trace Fork about 2 miles below the present site of Panther State Forest headquarters and just 3 1/2 miles from Camp Panther, P-65.

The primary work project for Camp Panther, during the summer of 1935, was the construction of a road up the hollow to the camp site. Problems, however, were encountered and cold weather arrived before the road could be completed to the camp. Therefore the camp was not approved for the sixth period (Oct. '35-Apr. '36). Orders came to close down the project and abandon Camp P-65, so the tent camp was razed October 19,1935.

The enrollees were distributed among other companies in the vicinity with 43 being transferred to Company 3543 in Camp McDowell. Capt. Jas. E. Wilkins and 2nd Lt. H. G. Williams were transferred to Camp P-64 and Wilkins placed in command of the camp. Camp Superintendent Luke Lilly and the rest of the technical staff transferred to other camps. Thus ended the brief existence of Camp Panther, P-65.

P-66, CAMP RALEIGH
9/14/35-1941

Located on private land in Raleigh County at Shady Springs on W. Va. Rt. 3 near the present site of Shady Springs High School, the camp was occupied September 14, 1935 by CCC Company 3531.

As with other forestry camps on private lands, the work projects involved forest fire protection activities.

It is not known when Camp Raleigh was closed, however an inspection report dated August 15, 1941 showed that it was in operation at that time. It is also known that the camp was authorized for the eighteenth period (Oct. '41-Mar. '42) so it can be assumed that it remained in operation at least until the end of 1941.

Capt. John J. Parker, Jr., 1st Lt. Bert W. Anderson, 1st Lt. A. Kramer and 1st Lt. Ben J. Peck were company commanders and R. C. Poore, F. H. Halstead, R. N. Dunkel and Donald L. Lord were camp superintendents.

S-67, CAMP WHITE SULPHUR
7/15/35-1941

This camp, which was sometimes referred to as Camp White Sulphur Springs, was located on Hart's Run in Greenbrier County on Greenbrier State Forest near the present site of forest headquarters and the swimming pool. Initially listed as P-67, the camp was later redesignated S-67 as work was concentrated on the development of Greenbrier State Forest.

The camp was established by an advance cadre from Company 549, Camp SCS-13 Ironton, Ohio, which had been quartered in tents, and was occupied July 15, 1935 by CCC Company 3512. A report dated October 19, 1935 advised that construction of camp buildings was 96% complete and the enrollees were in barracks and that all buildings had heat.

Since S-67 was not approved for the tenth period (Oct. '37-Mar. '38) it can be assumed that the camp was vacated for six months beginning about late fall of 1937. It was reoccupied June 1, 1938— this

28

time by CCC Company 1537 which had been transferred from Camp Seneca, S-51.

The exact date of closing is not known; however, the camp was not among the few CCC camps operating in the eighteenth period (Oct. '41-Mar '42). Since the last inspection report on file is dated August 8, 1940 it can be assumed that Camp S-67 remained open throughout the fall or early winter of 1940.

Capt. Houston C. Joyner was the company commander and the following were listed as camp superintendents: Raymond Parks, R. W. Griffiths, R. G. Thornburg and Barnes E. Hall.

In 1942, Camp White Sulphur was used as an assembly point for equipment, property and supplies, being brought in from abandoned CCC camps thereby providing a final service to the CCC.

P-68, CAMP PRICE
7/29/35-10/4/37

Located on Droop Mountain in Pocahontas County in what is now Droop Mountain Battlefield State Park the camp was on the site of the present park headquarters and service area. Several of the original camp buildings are still in use as park structures.

The camp was established with a cadre of 23 enrollees from Camp Seneca, S-51 and occupied July 29, 1935 by CCC Company 2598. The company was initially quartered in tents with construction of permanent quarters scheduled to start September 1, 1935. The camp buildings, of the portable type, were reported on October 8, 1935 to be 96% complete and with heat.

The major projects included reclaiming the battlefield, tree planting, construction of cabins, lookout tower and picnic area. Work on private land included construction of truck trails, telephone lines, fire breaks and ranger stations for forest fire protection.

Camp Price was abandoned October 4, 1937 and the portable buildings shipped to the 8th Corps Area, Quemada, New Mexico.

Capt. E. R. Howery was company commander and Hubert C. Kelly was camp superintendent.

P-69...

A state forestry camp was authorized but not funded so there was no construction.

P-70, CAMP MINGO
7/29/35-10/4/37

Camp Mingo was located in Mingo County about eight miles east of Delbarton on US Rt. 52 and Pigeon Creek at the mouth of Longtail Lick Branch at Musick, on the present site of Mingo Cable Service Inc. Camp Mingo was occupied July 29, 1935 by CCC Company 1579.

As with other forestry camps on private land in southern West Virginia the work mostly centered on forest fire control projects such as truck trail and telephone line construction and maintenance as well as actual forest fire suppression. A major project for Camp Mingo was the construction of a road to Mingo Mountain Fire Tower.

Since the camp was not approved for the tenth period (Oct. '37-Mar. '38) it was abandoned October 4, 1937 and the portable buildings transferred to Camp Kanawha, S-76, Charleston.

Company commanders included Capt. William F. Cahill, 1st Lt. H. M. Frink, and 1st Lt. Ben J. Peck. Camp superintendents were Don L. Cook and Robert L. Poore.

S-71, CAMP TWELVEPOLE (or ARACOMA)
7/13/35-4/5/37

Originally designated Camp P-71 for work on private forest land, it was redesignated S-71 when the camp was assigned work on Cabwaylingo State Forest along with Camp Anthony Wayne, S-61.

Located just across the Wayne County line in Mingo County at the mouth of Poor Branch of Twelvepole Creek, the camp was occupied July 13, 1935 by CCC Company 3540. A September 12, 1935 report indicated that construction of the camp buildings was 90% complete and that the enrollees were quartered in barracks. Work in the field had started August 8.

Work projects included fire control, forest stand improvement, recreation development, wildlife feeding, surveys and stream development.

The camp was not approved for the ninth period (Apr.-Aug. '37) so it was abandoned April 5, 1937 and the camp buildings were salvaged for CCC use.

Capt. C. B. Denman and Capt. Franklin W. Patton were company commanders and Daniel K. Flynn and A. A. Price were camp superintendents. Emory N. Wriston who later was recognized as a pioneer in conservation in West Virginia was senior foreman.

S-72, CAMP RANDOLPH
7/15/35-10/4/37

Camp Randolph was located in Randolph County near Elkwater and about one half mile north of the junction of the Kumbrabow State Forest road, County Route 16 with U. S. Route 219. The camp site is bisected by the present U. S. 219, however the original highway was to the west of the camp. A modern brick residence has been built around the original camp office building.

The camp was occupied July 15, 1935 by CCC Company 3520. A September 27, 1935 report advised that camp personnel were quartered in tents and that no building material had arrived. The buildings, when finally erected, were of the portable type.

Camp Randolph, although not on state forest property, was one of two CCC camps allocated for work on Kumbrabow State Forest. Originally designated P-72 it had been redesignated S-72 when it was assigned to work on the state forest.

The major work projects included fire hazard reduction, forest stand improvement, recreational development and wildlife surveys.

The camp was not approved for the tenth period (Oct. '37-Mar. '38) so it was abandoned October 4, 1937 and the buildings dismantled by the Army for use in constructing educational buildings and replacements in other camps.

Capt. Harold F. Thomas, Capt. Orville W. Rice, 1st Lt. Harold A. Staats and 1st Lt. Ely G. Fenton were company commanders and Donald L. Lord and J. Ligon Coyner were camp superintendents.

P-73, CAMP PRESTON
7/15/35-3/13/37

Camp Preston was located in Preston County about two miles southeast of Kingwood on the east side of Cheat River and just one fourth mile up county road 7/13 from WV Rt. 7. This camp, located on the present site of the Preston County Country Club, was occupied July 15, 1935 by CCC Company 3527.

A report dated September 25, 1935 advised that all enrollees were quartered in barracks, a bathhouse was under construction and erection of camp buildings was 65% complete.

Major work projects for the camp included fire hazard reduction, tree seed collecting, forest fire fighting and recreational development on Cooper's Rock State Forest about thirty-six miles away.

In addition to providing crews for work on the state forest, the base camp also maintained a side camp consisting of 65 men on Cooper's Rock State Forest.

Due to the distance between P-73 and its main work project, the condition of some of the roads traveled and the various problems associated with maintaining a side camp so distant, a request was made on September 12, 1936 that the camp and CCC company be moved to Cooper's Rock State Forest.

In response to this request, on or about March 13, 1937, Camp Preston was abandoned and the move made. One camp building was sold and the rest of them moved to Camp Rhododendron, S-75, Morgantown, along with the technical staff and all personnel of CCC Company 3527.

R. E. Jackson was camp superintendent and Capt. A. P. Lesnick was company commander.

P-74, CAMP WEBSTER
7/28/35-2/8/36

Camp Webster was located in Webster County about four miles northwest of Webster Springs on WV Routes 15 and 20. The camp was situated on land leased from Samuel Miller on the headwaters of Grassy Creek and about 800 feet to the right of the highway. The camp was occupied July 18,1935 by CCC Company 3504.

An inspection report dated September 30, 1935 stated that the enrollees were quartered in tents but were expected to be in barracks by October 2. Construction of camp buildings was reported to be 95% complete.

Forest protection including fire control work was the principal activity of the enrollees in Camp P-74.

The camp was not approved for the sixth period (Oct. '35-Mar. '36) so it was abandoned January 8, 1936 and the buildings salvaged for CCC use by the Army.

Capt. Stephen H. Hayward was the company commander and F. H. Halstead and R. L. Poore were camp superintendents.

S-75, CAMP RHODODENDRON
3/13/37-3/31/42

Located in Monongalia County near Cheat Lake on WV Route 857 and on Cooper's Rock State Forest, this camp was occupied March 13, 1937 by CCC Company 3527 which had been transferred from Camp Preston, P-73, Kingwood. The camp buildings were also moved from P-73 and all except the office building had been erected by April 19.

Work projects for the camp included building roads, trails, picnic shelters, two residences and other recreational facilities on Cooper's Rock State Forest. The enrollees were also engaged in fighting forest fires on both state and private lands in the area.

To complete its work projects, Camp Rhododendron continued to operate until the spring of 1942 when the camp was officially phased out on March 31, 1942 after being in operation for five years.

Capt. William W. Robinson, the first commanding officer for the camp was replaced by Capt. George R. Kyle in September 1937. Later company commanders included Capt. John P. West and Lt. Quinn L. Oldaker. During the life of Camp Rhododendron, Robert E. Jackson was the only camp superintendent.

S-76, CAMP KANAWHA
4/7/38-6/30/42

Located in Kanawha County in Shrewsbury Hollow of Davis Creek at the present site of the swimming pool in Kanawha State Forest, this camp was occupied April 7,1938 by CCC Company 2599 which had transferred from Camp Boone, P-55, Keith, W. Va.

The main project for the camp was the development of recreation facilities on Kanawha State Forest and the protection of the forest from fires. Roads, bridges, trails and telephone lines were built, picnic areas developed and several buildings constructed at forest headquarters.

On March 12, 1942 CCC Company 2599 was replaced by Company 1547V, a veterans company which had come from Camp Stonewall Jackson, SCS-12, Jane Lew. Then on June 15 Company 1547V was replaced by Company 3538C which came from Camp Carver, S-77, Panther, and remained for a few weeks until the conclusion of the CCC program June 30, 1942 or soon thereafter.

1st Lt. M. M. Brown was a company commander and Charles E. Barrett and C. Earl Mullins were camp superintendents.

S-77, CAMP CARVER
11/8/41-6/19/42

An initial purchase by the State of West Virginia of 4,877 acres of forest land on the watershed of Panther Creek in the western end of McDowell County September 30,1940 represented the beginning of Panther State Forest, initially called Panther Creek State Forest.

A CCC camp was authorized for the area for erection on Panther Creek, about a mile above the mouth of Trace Fork, the site of an earlier

CCC camp, Camp McDowell, P-64, which had been abandoned May 31, 1937 and the buildings disposed of long before the area came under state ownership.

The new camp, known as Camp Carver, S-77, consisted of all new buildings which had been erected in 1941 and occupied November 8,1941 by CCC Company 3538C, a junior colored company which was transferred from Camp War, P-63, Berwind, when that camp was abandoned.

The camp work projects were directed toward the development of Panther State Forest and the maintenance of the entrance road as well as forest fire protection. Following the occupation of the camp in November, little was accomplished on the project work until January except for the fighting of a forest fire in November. From January 1 through April 30, 7,411 man-days of labor were reported accomplished, most of which had been spent on the improvement of the camp entrance road. Not much more was accomplished by this camp since word was received in May that the camp was to be evacuated in June and the company transferred.

On June 19, 1942 Company 3538C was transferred to Camp Kanawha, S-76, Charleston and Camp S-77 was abandoned. The portable camp buildings were made available to the military and are reported to have been shipped to the South Pacific.

Later on, the buildings from Camp War, P-63 were transferred to the Camp Carver site and erected for use as a 4-H camp.

Walter Farmer was company commander and Martin L. Lilly was acting camp superintendent, during the short time Camp Carver was in operation.

Parsons Nursery, Civilian Conservation Corps Blacksmith Shop
— Library of Congress Reproduction Number HABS WVA,47-PARS.V,1R--1

W. VA. CONSERVATION COMMISSION
DIVISION OF STATE PARKS

The Division of State Parks of the Conservation Commission, which in 1961 became the Division of Parks and Recreation of the W. Va. Department of Natural Resources, was in 1934 responsible for the development of state park recreation facilities on several recently acquired properties. With the establishment of the CCC, development of these state parks areas became possible.

A total of nine CCC camps were authorized for work en West Virginia state parks, however only eight camps were established since Camp SP-9, scheduled for Tomlinson Run State Park, was not funded. One of the eight camps, Camp Waddington, SP-8, was en Oglebay Park which was started as a state park but was later turned over to the City of Wheeling.

Work projects on the various state parks included road and trail construction, installation of water and sewer systems, telephone and power line construction and the erection of cabins and other buildings, most of which involved "rustic" architecture with the use of logs, rustic woodwork and stone. The CCC enrollees also built picnic areas, swimming pools, game courts and other recreation facilities. They also fought forest fires when necessary.

SP-1, CAMP SEEBERT
5/15/34-3/5/37

Located on Greenbrier River at the mouth of Island Lick Run in Watoga State Park near the present site of park rental cabins No. 1 and 2, this camp was first occupied on Tuesday, May 15, 1934 by CCC Company 1541V. This company, consisting of 185 World War I veterans, under the command of Capt. Keith R. Smith, is believed to have come from Ohio. The veterans were quartered in tents throughout the summer pursuing their main project of erecting camp buildings including barracks.

On October 3, 1934 Company 1541V was replaced by Company 1535, a junior company which had transferred from Camp Pocahontas, P-56, Cass, W. Va.

The enrollees of Camp Seebert participated in the development of Watoga State Park, beginning with the Construction of a road from Beaver Creek to the Greenbrier River. This was followed by the construction of cabins, an office-restaurant building, the superintendent's residence and work on the dam. Camp personnel also built and operated the Current Run Ferry. When the camp closed, Camp Watoga took over and operated the ferry until the ferryboat sank in 1938.

When Camp Seebert closed March 5, 1937 the officers' quarters building was transferred to the park. It was remodeled and used as rental cabin No. 3 until it burned October 13,1987.

Capt. Smith, the first commanding officer, was replaced in the fall of 1934 by Capt. W. S. Wade. Later commanding officers were: Capt. Fred Klenk, 1st Lt. Russell E. Baker and Capt. M. N. Shreves. Boyd B. Hill was the camp superintendent.

SP-2, CAMP HARDY
5/15/34-1940

Located in Hardy County on Howard's Lick Run near the entrance to Lost River State Park the camp was occupied May 15, 1934 by CCC Company 1524 which had been transferred from Camp Leadmine, F-10, Leadmine, Tucker County.

The enrollees of this camp were involved in constructing cabins and other recreational facilities on Lost River State Park.

Capt. James G. Graham, Capt. Cyril Wilson, 1st Lt. William B. Cook and 1st Lt. Robert C. Simpson served as company commanders and Ira F. Kuhn, Thomas H. Olinger and Earl E. Kiser were camp superintendents.

The last camp inspection report en file is dated September 17,

1940 and the camp was not listed in the 1941 *W. Va. Blue Book* so it is believed that Camp Hardy was abandoned late in 1940.

SP-3, CAMP BEAVER
5/14/34-8/14/37

Located in Fayette County in Babcock State Park, across W. Va. Rt. 11 from the present park campground, the camp was occupied May 14,1934 by CCC Company 1522.

Camp Beaver was assigned projects for the development of recreational facilities en Babcock State Park, including the stone park administration building, the dam on Glade Creek and the nearby log vacation cabins. The camp also provided for the construction of the picnic shelter and museum building on Hawks Nest State Park, about 25 miles away.

Capt. John H. Enlow, 1st Lt. Glenn Myers, Capt. C. D. Riggle and Capt. A. S. Anderson were company commanders. James H. Baldwin, Boyd B. Hill and Edwin G. Davisson, Jr., were camp superintendents.

The camp was not approved for the tenth period (Oct. '37-Mar. '38) so it was abandoned August 14, 1937.

SP-4, CAMP MORGAN
10/4/34-1941

Located in what is now the main picnic area of Cacapon State Park in Morgan County, this camp was occupied October 4, 1934 by CCC Company 1523 which had been transferred from Camp Little Fork, F-8, Sugar Grove, W. Va.

The enrollees in Camp Morgan built log rental cabins and other recreational facilities on Cacapon State Park.

Capt. Thomas M. Barton, Capt. William H. Shields and 1st Lt. Charles W. Wilmore were company commanders and C. E. Dill, William H. Shields and Linn Wilson, who later became chief of state parks, were camp superintendents.

The last camp inspection report on file is dated July 14, 1941 and

the camp is not listed with those camps operating in the eighteenth
period (Oct. '41-Mar. '42) so it is believed that the camp was abandoned
in the fall of 1941.

SP-5, CAMP WATOGA
8/15/34-7/13/42

Originally established as S-52, a state forest camp, and occupied by
CCC Company 1525, June 18, 1933, Camp Watoga was redesignated
SP-5 as a state park camp en August 15, 1934, when Watoga became
a state park. It was located in what is now the maintenance area of
Watoga State Park.

This camp, along with Camp Seebert, SP-1, participated in park
development projects including construction of roads, trails, cabins, the
administration building and the building of a dam to form an eleven
acre lake. Light fixtures, hinges, door latches and fireplace sets for
the cabins were crafted in the camp blacksmith shop. The swimming
pool, started in 1939 and completed in 1940, was the last major project
completed by the camp.

During its time of operation, Camp Watoga was served by several
company commanders including Captain L. H. Headington, 1st Lt.
Thomas E. Virgin and Captain Harry I. Marks. Camp superintendents
included S. E. Neese, Grady Arbogast and Mortimer W. Gamble.

After the camp closed July 13, 1942, the buildings were transferred
to the state for park use. Several were used for storage for a few years
and later razed. By 1985 only four original CCC buildings remained
in service. The officers' quarters housed park personnel; the foremen's
quarters had become the park woodworking shop; the CCC garage, an
equipment storage building and the one remaining enrollees' barracks,
a storage building.

SP-6, CAMP LEE
7/10/35-1942

Located across the highway from Camp Beaver, SP-3 on the site of

the present campground in Babcock State Park, the camp was occupied
July 10, 1935 by CCC Company 532.

The enrollees of Camp Lee worked on the vacation cabins, picnic
areas, game courts and other recreational facilities as well as roads
and trails for Babcock State Park. Camp Lee also provided labor for
the construction of the concession building, public toilet building and
other facilities for Hawks Nest State Park about 25 miles from the camp.

Lt. (USNR) Earle D. Burson, Capt. John H. Enlow and 1st Lt.
Benjamin J. Peck were company commanders. James H. Baldwin, Boyd
B. Hill and Edwin G. Davisson, Jr. were camp superintendents.

When Babcock State Park was opened to the public July 1, 1937 Mr.
Baldwin was appointed park superintendent and Mr. Hill succeeded
him as camp superintendent.

The last camp inspection report on file is dated July 12, 1941,
however, since the camp was authorized for the eighteenth period (Oct.
'41-Mar. '42), it is believed that the camp was in operation until early
1942.

SP-7, CAMP WILL ROGERS
7/16/35-10/4/37

Located in Pocahontas County on Laurel Run in Burr Valley at
the south entrance to Watoga State Park, this camp was occupied July
16, 1935 by CCC Company 3537 after being established by an advance
cadre of 23 enrollees from Camp SP-4, London, Ky. who were quartered
in tents.

An inspection report of August 5, 1935 reported that construction
had started on the camp buildings but they were only about 15%
complete. The buildings were being erected by local carpenters.

Camp SP-7 had been established for the purpose of developing
a recreation complex in the southern section of Watoga State Park,
including construction of a dam across Laurel Run to create a forty acre
lake. A nationwide reduction in the CCC program, however, resulted
in this camp, along with many others, being disapproved for the
tenth period (Oct. '37-Mar. '38) so Camp Will Rogers was abandoned

October 4, 1937 and the camp buildings transferred to the Army for use as educational buildings in other camps. This forced the abandonment of the Laurel Run project.

Uncompleted projects started by Camp Will Rogers were turned over to Camp Watoga which was located nearby in Watoga State Park.

Capt. Russell L. Schoene was company commander and Sidney E. Neese was camp superintendent.

SP-8, CAMP WADDINGTON
7/19/35-7/8/37

Located in Ohio County five miles northwest of Wheeling en W. Va. Route 44 in what is now Oglebay Park, Camp Waddington was occupied July 19, 1935 by CCC Company 3529. Initially listed as Oglebay State Park, then changed to Oglebay Metropolitan Park, the area subsequently became Oglebay Park and was administered by the Wheeling Park Commission.

For the two years that it was in operation, Camp SP-8 provided labor for the construction of recreational facilities on Oglebay Park.

Since the camp was not approved for the tenth period (Oct. '37-Mar. '38) it was abandoned July 8, 1937 and the buildings transferred to the Wheeling Park Commission.

Capt. George R. Kyle was company commander and W. W. Kinsley and C. E. Dill were camp superintendents.

SP-9, Chester, W. Va.

A state park camp was authorized for Tomlinson Run State Park in Hancock County, but by some reports, was neither funded nor built. One source, however, Perry Merrill in Roosevelt's Forest Army states that a camp was built at the Tomlinson Run site in 1941 but was never occupied.

Ca. 1935. View East, CCC Camp Parsons, Forest Service Truck Storage On Left,
Water Tank (Demolished), Mess Hall (Demolished).
— Library of Congress Reproduction Number HABS WVA,47-PARS.V,1Q--3

U. S. DEPARTMENT OF AGRICULTURE
SOIL CONSERVATION SERVICE

The Soil Erosion Service was established in 1933 under the Department of the Interior, but in 1935 was transferred to the Department of Agriculture and the name changed to the Soil Conservation Service. Its main purpose was to help farmers use land and water resources to reduce flood and erosion loss. It was responsible for flood prevention, drainage and watershed protection.

In West Virginia twelve CCC camps were authorized for the Soil Conservation Service. Eleven were actually established for work on farms, usually within a twenty mile radius of the camp. Work projects included gully control, tree planting, tile drains, pond construction, surveying for contour farming and other work related to erosion control.

The first two camps were established in 1934 as SES-1, Camp Roane and SES-2, Camp Crawford. These camps were redesignated as SCS-1 and SCS-2 when the Soil Erosion Service was changed to the Soil Conservation Service in 1935.

SCS-1 (Originally SES-1), CAMP ROANE
10/10/34-1/10/36

Camp Roane was located in Roane County between Spencer and Reedy and three-fourths of a mile north of Billings. Situated east of WV Rt. 14 and Reedy Creek and just north of the mouth of Miller Run, the camp was about five miles northeast of Spencer on the site now occupied by the Burke-Parsons-Bowlby Corporation's timber treating plant.

The camp was established September 18, 1934 by an advance cadre and was occupied October 10 by CCC Company 1547V, a veterans' company comprised of World War I veterans, which had been transferred from Camp Oak Hill, P-60. Originally designated SES-1 by the Soil Erosion Service, the camp was redesignated SCS-1 when the agency's name was changed to Soil Conservation Service.

Erection of the camp buildings, which had begun September 18, 1934, was completed January 23, 1935.

As with other Soil Conservation Service camps, the enrollees did erosion control work on private farms. This included projects such as preparation of farm plans, surveying for contour farming and construction of ponds and diversion ditches.

The camp was not approved for the sixth period (Oct. '35-Mar. '36) so CCC Company 1547V was transferred to Camp Jackson, SCS-6, Ripley, on January 10, 1936 and the camp was placed on a maintenance basis July 1, 1936. Ownership of the camp buildings was transferred to Roane County.

Capt. George R. Kyle and Capt. James L. Harvey were company commanders and Robert L. Porter was camp superintendent.

SCS-2 (Originally SES-2), CAMP CRAWFORD
5/17/34-7/31/39

Located in Wirt County at the north edge of Elizabeth on the bottom land site between WV Rt. 14 and the Little Kanawha River, this camp was occupied May 17, 1934 by CCC Company 1512. The camp was named for a CCC enrollee leader of the original cadre from Indiana that set up the camp. This is the only known case in West Virginia of a camp being named for an enrollee.

General conservation work was performed on private lands in a twenty mile radius of the camp.

Camp Crawford was abandoned July 31, 1939 and Company 1512 was transferred to Camp Cabell, SCS-10, Milton.

Capt. Albert J. Aylor, Capt. Frank H. Tomkies, 1st Lt. Adolph M. Edwards, 1st Lt. Harold B. Fisher and 1st Lt. Bert W. Anderson served as company commanders and H. G. Debald and Harry C. Wolfe were camp superintendents.

SCS-3, CAMP MARSHALL
7/15/35-1941

Located in Marshall County just outside and northeast of Moundsville on Middle Grave Creek, this camp was occupied July 15, 1935 by CCC Company 3508. Water service for the camp was received from the City of Moundsville.

Camp SCS-3 was the parent camp of two large side camps, SCS-12 at Jane Lew and SP-9 at New Cumberland.

The enrollees in Camp Marshall built stream embankments, burned and spread lime, built fences, planted trees and performed other tasks to improve farmlands.

Company commanders included 1st Lt. Glen R. Myers, 1st Lt. Hicks M. Frink and 2nd Lt. Harry E. Sturms. Camp superintendents were Charles H. Lloyd, Leland D. Brown, Louis C. Linkous, Frank O. Leonard and H. G. Debald.

The last inspection report dated August 26, 1941 stated that Camp SCS-3 was supposed to have been abandoned prior to that date and that it was no longer on the records. It further stated that the camp was still occupied as a full service camp and the parent camp for two side camps. Another report stated that the camp was originally scheduled for closing in June 1941 but because the new camp, probably Camp Stonewall Jackson, was not ready, Company 3508 remained at Camp Marshall until October. It seems likely that Company 3508 was disbanded and Camp Marshall abandoned about October 1, 1941.

SCS-4, CAMP ROWAN
8/13/35-1/10/40

Camp Rowan was located in Monroe County about a mile south of Union on the east side of the Willow Bend road, County Route 13. It was occupied August 13, 1935 by CCC Company 3549. An October 12, 1935 inspection report indicated that the men were quartered in tents and that construction of the camp buildings, of the portable type, was 30% complete.

Camp Rowan was named for a Gap Mills native, Andrew Summers Rowan (1857-1943), the U. S. Army officer who carried President McKinley's message to the Cuban rebel, General Garcia in 1898.

The camp enrollees performed soil erosion control work on local farms as was done by similar SCS camps throughout the state.

Captains J. T. Smoody, A. M. Emerson and Arnett S. Anderson and 1st Lt. Gordon R. Willis were company commanders and Louis C. Linkous and Leland D. Brown were camp superintendents.

Camp Rowan was abandoned January 10, 1940 and CCC Company 3549 was transferred to a new camp, Camp Fairfax, SCS-11, Hedgesville in Berkeley County.

SCS-5, CAMP LEWIS
8/19/35-1941

Located in Greenbrier County about two miles north of Lewisburg just east of U. S. Rt. 219 on County Rt. 38, this camp was established July 29, 1935 by a cadre of 23 men from Camp PE-77, Company 532, Mac Arthur, Ohio. CCC Company 3510, in full strength, occupied Camp Lewis August 19, and was quartered in tents until construction of the camp buildings was completed later in the fall.

The enrollees worked on soil erosion control projects on farms in the area.

Capt. Joseph C. Oxley, 2nd Lt. Philip A. Staub, 2nd Lt. Austin M. Henderson and 2nd Lt. Kenneth F. Fatkin were company commanders and W. Fred Porter was the camp superintendent.

The last inspection report was dated August 9, 1940, however, Camp Lewis was listed with the camps in operation for the eighteenth period (Oct. '41-Mar. '42) so it is believed that the camp probably remained in service until fall of 1941 or later.

Early in 1942 a side camp was authorized by the Army to occupy the evacuated Camp Lewis to provide personnel to handle the equipment, property and supplies being brought in to Camp White Sulphur, S-67 for the Army.

SCS-6, CAMP JACKSON
8/30/35-11/15/41

Located in Jackson County in the Town of Ripley, near the present site of Ripley High School, this camp was occupied August 30, 1935 by CCC Company 1580. An inspection report dated August 20, 1935 advised that this was still a tent camp since materials had not yet been received for the camp buildings. It is believed that new buildings, of the portable type, were erected and occupied by late fall or early winter.

On or about January 11, 1936 Company 1580 was replaced by a company of veterans, Company 1547V, which had transferred from Camp Roane, SCS-1, Reedy, W. Va.

Capt. George R. Kyle, Capt. James G. Harvey, Capt. Henry F. Gravenkemper and 1st Lt. Hicks M. Frink were company commanders and Roy D. Bradley was camp superintendent.

On November 13, 1941 Camp Jackson was abandoned and CCC Company 1547V was transferred to Camp Stonewall Jackson, SCS-12 at Jane Lew.

SCS-7, CAMP HARRISON
7/10/35-12/15/37

Camp Harrison was located in Harrison County about three miles southeast of Clarksburg at Quiet Dell on WV Rt. 20. The camp was occupied July 10, 1935 by CCC Company 2592. The camp site would have been in the vicinity of the point where I-79 crosses WV Rt. 20. The last remaining camp buildings were removed with the construction of 1-79.

As with other SCS camps, the enrollees performed soil erosion control work on private farms in the area.

On or about September 10, 1937 eleven members of the technical staff were transferred to other camps and Camp SCS-7 ceased operations. Two staff members remained as custodians of the vacated camp. At this point it was suggested that the camp be turned into a receiving hospital for tubercular patients. This proposal, however, was dropped when it became apparent that funds were not available for such a project.

The camp was totally abandoned December 15, 1937 and five of the camp buildings were transferred to the Soil Conservation Service for CCC use. The remaining buildings, of the portable type, were shipped to the Eighth Corps Area (DG-101), Bloomfield, NM for army use.

Capt. Burtch W. Beall and Capt. Virgil E. Burriss were company commanders and F. O. Leonard was the camp superintendent.

SCS-8, CAMP TYGART
9/14/35-1942

Camp Tygart was located in Randolph County on County Route 21, one and a fourth miles south of its intersection, in Dailey, with U. S. Route 219. The camp, being situated at the edge of the Tygart Valley Homestead, utilized its water and sewage systems. The camp site is now occupied by a housing development.

This SCS camp was occupied September 14, 1935 by CCC Company 2584. As of September 28 the men were still quartered in tents since the material for constructing the camp buildings had not been received. It is believed that the camp buildings were constructed and occupied late in the fall or early winter. The camp personnel were involved in soil erosion control projects on private farms in the vicinity.

Capt. Orville W. Rice, 1st Lt. Robert M. Richey and 2nd Lt. Eli M. Dews were company commanders and Leon Silberberger was camp superintendent.

The last camp inspection report on file was dated July 17, 1941 and Camp Tygart was listed with the camps operating in the eighteenth period (Oct. '41-Mar. "42) so the camp probably was not abandoned until the spring of 1942.

SCS-9. . .

A Soil Conservation Service camp was assigned to Monongalia County but was canceled before construction was started.

SCS-10, CAMP CABELL
7/31/39-6/1/41

Camp Cabell was located in Cabell County about two miles east of Milton on bottom land of the Berkeley farm, south of US Rt. 60 and between the highway and the railroad tracks. Due to its location, the camp was able to obtain water service from the Town of Milton. The camp was occupied July 31, 1939 by CCC Company 1512 which had been transferred from Camp Crawford, SCS-2, Elizabeth.

Work on local farms included fence construction, gully treatment, surveying and land preparation for strip cropping. A major project was the construction of a dam, creating a one acre pond, about a mile southeast of Milton on county Rt. 25.

H. B. Fisher and Homer G. Da vies were company commanders and H. G. Debald was camp superintendent.

The last inspection report was dated August 2, 1940, however, it is believed that the camp remained in operation until May or June of 1941. The camp buildings were dismantled in September and October of that year.

SCS-11, CAMP FAIRFAX
1/11/40-5/25/42

Located in Berkeley County three miles west of Hedgesville on the south side of WV Rt. 9 near its junction with county Rt. 23, Camp Fairfax was occupied January 11, 1940 by CCC Company 3549 which had transferred from Camp Rowan, SCS-4, Union. The camp was named for the Fairfaxes of Virginia from whom the camp superintendent, Leland Brown claimed descent.

Camp personnel were engaged in aiding farmers in applying conservation measures to their farms. This included tree planting, fence building, construction of diversion ditches and terraces, quarrying and burning limestone, construction of contour furrows, small reservoirs, check dams and terrace outlets. The enrollees also fought forest fires when necessary.

An inspection report indicated that the camp was scheduled to be abandoned May 25, 1942, which apparently it was.

Elmore K. Fabrick and A. M. Anderson were company commanders and Leland D. Brown and Norris R. Caryl were camp superintendents.

SCS-12, CAMP STONEWALL JACKSON
11/15/41-6/30/42

Located in Lewis County on US Rt. 19 about one mile northwest of Jane Lew and near the Harrison County line, this camp was occupied November 15,1941 by CCC Company 1547V, a veterans' company which had been transferred from Camp Jackson, SCS-6, Ripley. On March 12, 1942 Company 1547V was transferred to Camp Kanawha, S-76, Charleston and on March 16 Company 2590 came to Camp Stonewall Jackson from Camp Anthony, F-18, Neola, Greenbrier County.

Company 2590 was disbanded about June 14 and all members and funds were transferred to Company 1525 located at Camp Watoga, SP-5. Company 1547V was then ordered back to Camp Stonewall Jackson from Camp Kanawha.

Since funds were not appropriated to extend the CCC, the Corps went out of existence June 30, 1942. It can therefore be assumed that Camp SCS-12 was abandoned June 30 along with all other camps still in operation.

William F. Owen and Sewell Fisher were company commanders and W. Fred Porter was camp superintendent during the short existence of Camp Stonewall Jackson.

Parsons Nursery, Civilian Conservation Corps Garage
— Library of Congress Reproduction Number HABS WVA,47-PARS.V,1Q--1

WAR DEPARTMENT ARMY CORPS OF ENGINEERS

The Corps of Engineers used CCC camps on several major flood control projects in other states, however only one camp was established by the Corps in West Virginia and that one was in operation for only fifteen months on Bluestone Reservoir property.

C of E-1, CAMP BLUESTONE
12/4/35-3/3/37

Located in Summers County adjacent to the City of Hinton and below Bluestone Reservoir dam, this camp was occupied December 4, 1935 by CCC Company 524 which had been transferred from Camp Alvon, F-14, Alvon, W. Va.

The primary project for the camp was cutting right of way on the Bluestone Reservoir area.

After being in operation for fifteen months, Camp Bluestone was abandoned March 3, 1937 and the camp buildings shipped to the Ninth Corps Area, Harper, Oregon.

NOTE:

The writer, a 1939 graduate of the West Virginia University Forestry School had some experience with the CCC program, having worked as a student aide in Camp Lewis, Lewisburg during the summer of 1936 and as a squad foreman in Camp Rhododendron, Morgantown and Camp Bowers, Pickens during 1940 and 1941.

Main Floor, North Room, Looking North.
Parsons Nursery, Civilian Conservation Corps Garage
— Library of Congress Reproduction Number HABS WVA,47-PARS.V,1Q--2

APPENDIX A

CIVILIAN CONSERVATION CORPS (CCC) CAMPS
IN WEST VIRGINIA 1933–1942

United States Forest Service

Camp	Company	Dates	Counties
F-1, Camp Dry Fork	519	5/20/33-11/18/33	Tucker
F-2, Camp Glady Fork	524	5/26/33-11/10/34	Randolph
	566	6/14/35-1/1/38	
F-3, Camp Parsons	518	5/20/33-1942	Tucker
F-4, Camp Laurel Fork	520	5/20/33-7/10/37	Randolph
F-5, Camp Circleville	523	5/26/33-11/10/33	Pendleton
F-6, Camp Thornwood	521	5/23/33-11/20/33	Pocahontas
	2586	7/1/35-1942	
F-7, Camp Wolf Gap	333	5/15/33-3/24/34	Hardy
F-8, Camp Little Fork	2587	4/1/35-12/15/37	Pendleton
F-9, Camp Randolph (1st)	525	5/26/33-11/20/33	Randolph
F-10, Camp Leadmine	1524	6/18/33-5/15/34	Tucker
F-11, Camp North Fork	519	11/18/33-10/1/41	Grant
F-12, Camp Woodbine	521	11/20/33-10/23/35	Nicholas
F-13, Camp Cranberry	525	11/20/33-1/1/42	Webster
F-14, Camp Alvon	524	11/10/34-12/4/35	Greenbrier
F-15, Camp Black Mountain	2589	7/11/35-3/1/39	Pocahontas
	2590	5/10/41-11/1/41	
F-16, Camp Nicholas	2591	7/1/35-1/8/36	Webster
F-17, Camp Copperhead	3539	7/10/35-10/4/37	Pocahontas

F-18, Camp Anthony	2570	8/19/35-5/9/41	Greenbrier
	2570	11/1/41-3/15/42	
F-19, Camp Loring	2596	7/25/35-1/11/36	Pocahontas
	1580	1/11/36-10/4/37	
F-20, Camp White	2595	7/1/35-10/4/37	Pendleton
F-21 *(Authorized but not funded nor established)*			Pocahontas
F-22, Camp Hutton	2597	7/10/35-1938	Randolph
F-23, Camp Cheat Mountain	2586	7/11/40-10/1/40	Randolph
(summer camp)	2586	5/19/41-10/1/41	
F-24, Camp Scott	519	7/11/40-11/1/40	Randolph
(summer camp)	519	4/16/41-11/14/41	

W. Va. Division of Forestry

S-51, Camp Seneca	1537	6/22/33-5/31/38	Pocahontas
S-52, Camp Watoga	1525	6/18/33-8/15/34	Pocahontas
P-53, Camp Nicholas	1547V	7/18/33-5/15/34	Webster
P-54, Camp Wyoming	1538	6/22/33-4/30/36	Wyoming
P-55, Camp Boone	1540	6/22/33-10/3/34	Boone
	2599	7/2/35-4/7/38	
P-56, Camp Pocahontas	1535	6/23/33-10/4/34	Pocahontas
	2588	7/1/35-10/28/35	
P-57, Camp Greenbrier	1539	6/23/33-8/30/35	Greenbrier
	2593	7/1/35-1/11/36	
P-58, Camp Logan	1558V	7/18/33-10/20/38	Logan
	1558V	4/11/39-11/15/41	
P-59, Camp Kanawha	523	11/10/33-10/1/34	Kanawha
	3513	7/1/35-1/8/36	
P-60, Camp Oak Hill	1547V	5/15/34-10/10/34	Fayette
S-61, Camp Anthony Wayne	3532	7/4/35-10/20/38	Wayne
	1558V	10/20/38-4/11/39	
S-62, Camp Bowers	2594	7/1/35-1941	Randolph
P-63, Camp War	3538C	7/11/35-11/8/41	McDowell
P-64, Camp Mcdowell	3543	7/25/35-5/31/37	McDowell

P-65, Camp Panther	3534	4/1/35-10/19/35	McDowell
P-66, Camp Raleigh	3531	9/14/35-1/1/42	Raleigh
P-67, Camp White Sulphur	3512	7/15/35-10/1/37	Greenbrier
S-67, Camp White Sulphur	1537	6/1/38-1941	
P-68, Camp Price	2598	7/29/35-10/4/37	Pocahontas
P-69 *(Authorized but not funded nor established)*			
P-70, Camp Mingo	1579	7/29/35-10/4/37	Mingo
S-71, Camp Twelvepole	3540	7/13/35-4/5/37	Mingo
S-72, Camp Randolph	3520	7/15/35-10/4/37	Randolph
P-73, Camp Preston	3527	7/15/35-3/13/37	Preston
P-74, Camp Webster	3504	7/18/35-1/8/36	Webster
S-75, Camp Rhododendron	3527	3/13/37-3/31/42	Monogalia
S-76, Camp Kanawha	2599	4/7/38-11/15/41	Kanawha
	1547V	3/12/42-6/15/42	
	3538C	6/19/42-6/30/42	
S-77, Camp Carver	3538C	11/8/41-6/19/42	McDowell

W. Va. Division of State Parks

SP-1, Camp Seebert	1541V	5/15/34-10/3/34	Pocahontas
SP-1, Camp Seebert	1535	10/4/34-3/5/37	
SP-2, Camp Hardy	1524	5/15/34-1940	Hardy
SP-3, Camp Beaver	1522	5/14/34-8/14/37	Fayette
SP-4, Camp Morgan	1523	10/4/34-1941	Morgan
SP-5, Camp Watoga	1525	8/15/34-7/13/42	Pocahontas
SP-6, Camp Lee	532	7/10/35-1/1/42	Fayette
SP-7, Camp Will Rogers	3537	7/16/35-10/4/37	Pocahontas
SP-8, Camp Waddington	3529	7/19/35-7/8/37	Ohio
SP-9 *(Authorized but not funded nor established)*			Hancock

United States Soil Conservation Service

SCS-1, Camp Roane	1547V	10/10/34-1/10/36	Roane
SCS-2, Camp Crawford	1512	5/17/34-7/31/39	Wirt
SCS-3, Camp Marshall	3508	7/15/35-1941	Marshall
SCS-4, Camp Rowan	3549	8/13/35-1/10/40	Monroe

SCS-5, Camp Lewis	3510	7/29/35-1942	Greenbrier
SCS-6, Camp Jackson	1580	8/14/35-1/11/36	Jackson
	1547V	1/11/36-11/15/41	Jackson
SCS-7, Camp Harrison	2592	7/10/35-12/15/37	Harrison
SCS-8, Camp Tygart	2584	9/15/35-1941	Randolph
SCS-9 *(Authorized but not funded nor established)*			Monogalia
SCS-10, Camp Cabell	1512	7/31/39-6/1/41	Cabell
SCS-11, Camp Fairfax	3549	1/10/40-5/25/42	Berkeley
SCS-12, Camp Stonewall	1547V	11/15/41-3/12/42	Lewis
Jackson	2590	3/16/42-6/15/42	
	1547V	6/15/42-6/30/42	

United States Army — Corps of Engineers

C Of E-1, Camp Bluestone	524	12/4/35-3/3/37	Summers

Compiled from records in the National Archives, the W. Va.
Conservation Commission annual reports and *W. Va. Blue Books.*

Wash house on left, nursery office on right. - Parsons nursery
— Library of Congress Reproduction Number HABS WVA,47-PARS.V,1F- WV0386-1

APPENDIX B

CIVILIAN CONSERVATION CORPS (CCC) COMPANIES AND CAMPS IN WEST VIRGINIA 1933–1942

CCC Co.	Camp Name & No.	Address	Dates Occupied
518	Camp Parson, F-3	Parsons	5/20/33 - 1941
519	Camp Dry Fork, F-1	Davis	5/20/33 - 11/18/33
	Camp North Fork, F-11	Petersburg	11/18/33 - 10/1/41*
	Camp Scott, F-24	Whitmer	7/11/40 - 11/1/40
		(Summer Camp)	4/16/41 - 11/14/41
520	Camp Laurel Fork, F-4	Glady	5/20/33 - 7/10/37
521	Camp Thornwood, F-6	Durbin	5/23/33 - 11/20/33
	Camp Woodbine, F-12	Richwood	11/20/33 - 10/23/35
523	Camp Circleville, F-5	Circleville	5/26/33 - 11/10/33
	Camp Kanawha, P-59	Decota	11/10/33 - 10/1/34
524	Camp Glady Fork, F-2	Alpena	5/26/33 - 11/10/34
	Camp Alvon, F-14	Alvon	11/10/34 - 12/4/35
	Camp Bluestone, C of E-1	Hinton	12/4/35 - 3/3/37
525	Camp Randolph, (1st), F-9	Elkins	5/26/33 - 11/20/33
	Camp Cranberry, F-13	Dyer	11/20/33 - 1/1/42*
532	Camp Lee, SP-6	Clifftop	7/10/35 - 1/1/42*
566	Camp Glady Fork, F-2	Alpena	6/14/35 - 1/1/38
1512	Camp Crawford, SCS-2	Elizabeth	5/17/34 - 7/31/39
	Camp Cabell, SCS-10	Milton	7/31/39 - 6/1/41
1522	Camp Beaver, SP-3	Clifftop	5/14/34 - 8/14/37
1523	Camp Little Fork, F-8	Sugar Grove	6/18/33 - 10/4/34

	Camp Morgan, SP-4	Berkeley Springs	10/4/34 - 1941
1524	Camp Leadmine, F-10	Lead Mine	6/18/33 - 5/15/34
	Camp hardy, SP-2	Mathias	5/15/34 - 1940
1525	Camp Watoga, S-52 & SP-5	Huntersville	6/18/33 - 7/13/42
1535	Camp Pocahontas, P-56	Cass	6/23/33 - 10/4/34
	Camp Seebert, SP-1	Seebert	10/4/34 - 3/5/37
1537	Camp Seneca, S-51	Huntersville	6/22/33 - 5/31/38
	Camp White Sulphur, S-67	White Sulphur Springs	6/1/38 - 1941
1538	Camp Wyoming, P-54	Pineville	6/22/33 - 4/30/36
1539	Camp Greenbrier	Rupert	6/23/33 - 8/30/35
1540	Camp Boone, P-55	Keith	6/22/33 - 10/3/34
1541V	Camp Seebert, SP-1	Seebert	5/15/34 - 10/3/34
1547V	Camp Nicholas, P-53	Cowen	7/18/33 - 5/15/34
	Camp Oak Hill, P-60	Oak Hill	5/15/34 - 10/10/34
	Camp Roane, SCS-1	Reedy	10/10/34 - 1/10/36
	Camp Jackson, SCS-6	Ripley	1/11/36 - 11/15/41
	Camp Stonewall Jackson, SCS-12	Jane Lew	11/15/41 - 3/12/42
	Camp Kanawha, S-76	Charleston	3/12/42 - 6/15/42
	Camp Stonewall Jackson, SCS-12	Jane Lew	6/15/42 - 6/30/42
1558V	Camp Logan, P-58	Sharples	7/18/33 - 10/20/38
	Camp Anthony Wayne, S-61	Missouri Branch	10/20/38 - 4/11/39
	Camp Logan, P-58	Sharples	4/11/39 - 11/15/41
1579	Camp Mingo, P-70	Delbarton	7/29/35 - 10/4/37
1580	Camp Jackson, SCS-6	Ripley	8/14/35 - 1/11/36
	Camp Loring, F-19	Minnehaha Springs	1/11/36 - 10/4/37
2584	Camp Tygart, SCS-8	Beverly	9/15/35 - 1942
2586	Camp Thornwood, F-6	Durbin	7/1/35 - 1942
	Camp Cheat Mountain, F-23	Durbin	7/11/40 - 10/1/40
		(Summer Camp)	5/19/41 - 10/1/41
2587	Camp Little Fork, F-8	Sugar Grove	4/1/35 - 12/15/37
2588	Camp Pocahontas, P-56	Cass	7/1/35 - 10/28/35
2589	Camp Black Mountain, F-15	Marlinton	7/11/35 - 3/1/39
2590	Camp Anthony, F-13	Neola	8/19/35 - 5/9/41
	Camp Black Mountain, F-15	Marlinton	5/10/41 - 11/1/41*

	Camp Anthony, F-18	Neola	11/1/41 - 3/15/42
	Camp Stonewall Jackson, SCS-12	Jane Lew	3/16/42 - 6/15/42
2591	Camp Nicholas, F-16	Dyer	7/1/35 - 1/8/36
2592	Camp Harrison, SCS-7	Nutter Fort	7/10/35 - 12/15/37
2593	Camp Greenbrier, P-57	Rupert	7/1/35 - 1/11/36
2594	Camp Bowers, S-62	Pickens	7/1/35 - 1941
2595	Camp White, F-20	Onego	7/1/35 - 10/4/37
2596	Camp Loring, F-19	Minnehaha Springs	7/25/35 - 1/11/36
2597	Camp Hutton, F-22	Huttonsville	7/10/35 - 1938
2598	Camp Price, P-68	Hillsboro	7/29/35 - 10/4/37
2599	Camp Boone, P-55	Keith	7/2/35 - 4/7/38
	Camp Kanawha, S-76	Charleston	4/7/38 - 11/15/41
3504	Camp Webster, P-74	Webster Springs	7/18/35 - 1/8/36
3508	Camp Marshall, SCS-3	Moundsville	7/15/35 - 1941
3510	Camp Lewis, SCS-5	Lewisburg	7/29/35 - 1942
3512	Camp White Sulphur, S-67	White Sulphur Springs	7/15/35 - 10/1/37
3513	Camp Kanawha, P-59	Decota	7/1/35 - 1/8/36
3520	Camp Randolph, S-72	Elkwater	7/15/35 - 10/4/37
3527	Camp Preston, P-73	Kingwood	7/15/35 - 3/13/37
	Camp Rhododendron, S-75	Morgantown	3/13/37 - 3/31/42
3529	Camp Waddington, SP-8	Wheeling	7/19/35 - 7/8/37
3531	Camp Raleigh, P-66	Beckley	9/14/35 - 1/1/42*
3532	Camp Anthony Wayne, S-61	Missouri Branch	7/4/35 - 10/20/38
3534	Camp Panther, P-65	Panther	4/1/35 - 10/19/35
3537	Camp Will Rogers, SP-7	Seebert	7/16/35 - 10/4/37
3538C	Camp War, P-63	Berwind	7/11/35 - 11/8/41
	Camp Carver, S-77	Panther	11/8/41 - 6/19/42
	Camp Kanawha, S-76	Charleston	6/19/42 - 6/30/42
3539	Camp Copperhead, F-17	Frost	7/10/35 - 10/4/37
3540	Camp Twelvepole, S-71	Missouri Branch	7/13/35 - 4/5/37
3543	Camp McDowell, P-64	Panther	7/25/35 - 5/31/37
3549	Camp Rowan, SCS-4	Union	8/13/35 - 1/10/40
	Camp Fairfax, SCS-11	Hedgesville	1/10/40 - 5/25/42

* Approximate date

The first three digits and the second digit of four digit CCC company numbers denote the Army Corps Area in which the company was formed. West Virginia along with Ohio, Indiana, and Kentucky comprised the Fifth Corps Area.

A "V" following the company number denotes a veteran's company and a "C" denotes a colored company. The three companies in West Virginia carrying these designations are: 1547V, 1558V and 3538C.

Agencies in West Virginia sponsoring CCC camps:

W.Va. Conservation Commission, Division of Forestry	**P & S camps**
W.Va. Conservation Commission, Division of State Parks	**SP camps**
U.S. Forest Service	**F camps**
U.S. Soil Conservation Service	**SCS camps**
U.S. Army, Corps of Engineers	**C of E camps**

Parsons Nursery Bunkhouse
— Library of Congress Reproduction Number HABS WVA,47-PARS.V,1N--1

APPENDIX C

DISTRIBUTION OF CCC CAMPS BY COUNTY

County	F Camps	P&S Camps	SP Camps	SCS Camps	CE Camps	TOTAL
Pocahontas*	4	4	3			11*
Randolph	6	2		1		9
Greenbrier	2	2		1		5
McDowell		4				4
Webster*	2	2				4*
Fayette		1	2			3
Pendelton	3					3
Tucker	3					3
Hardy	1**		1			2**
Kanawha		2				2
Wayne		1				1
Berkeley				1		1
Boone		1				1
Cabell				1		1
Grant	1					1
Harrison				1		1
Jackson				1		1

County	F Camps	P&S Camps	SP Camps	SCS Camps	CE Camps	TOTAL
Lewis				1		1
Logan		1				1
Marshall				1		1
Mingo		2				2
Monongalia		1				1
Monroe				1		1
Morgan			1			1
Nicholas	1					1
Ohio			1			1
Preston		1				1
Raleigh		1				1
Roane				1		1
Summers					1	1
Wirt				1		1
Wyoming		1				1
TOTAL	23	26	8	11	1	69

* One camp site carries two camp designations.
** One camp was transferred to the State of Virginia.

CAMP DESIGNATIONS:
F = U.S. Forest Service
P&S = W.Va. Conservation Commission, Division of Forestry Camps
SP = W.Va. Conservation Commission, Division of State Parks Camps
SCS = U.S. Soil Conservation Camps
CE = U.S. Army Corps of Engineers Camps

For those wanting more information about the Civilian Conservation Corps, nationwide, the following profusely illustrated book is suggested: *The Tree Army* by Stan Cohen, Pictorial Histories publishing Company, 1980.

Bunk Room, Parsons Nursery Bunkhouse
— Library of Congress Reproduction Number HABS WVA,47-PARS.V,1N--4

SATURDAY NIGHT

Saturday night on the streets of Swago
And the C.C.C.'s are here
Strolling down to Slaven's poolroom
For their weekly beer.
Nails all clipped and their zipper jackets
Fastened up to the chin. . . .
Oh, girls come out in your Roebuck rayons
For the Army's in!

Saturday night and the C.C. Truckers
Stepping upon the gas. . . .
Out of the road if your life is precious
And let them pass.
Up and down by the commerce building
Taunting the bourgeoisie. . . .
No sleep tonight, for the Brush Hook Legions
Are on a spree.

Louise McNeill
Poet Laureate of West Virginia